Harnessing the Transformative Power of Positive Thinking

Harnessing the Transformative Power of Positive Thinking

By

Ruchi

Vij Books

New Delhi (India)

Published by

Vij Books
(Publishers, Distributors & Importers)
4836/24, 3rd Floor, Ansari Road
Delhi – 110 002
Phone: 91-11-43596460
Mobile: 98110 94883
e-mail: contact@vijpublishing.com
www.vijbooks.in

ISBN: 978-93-95675-93-2

Contents

Introduction: Exploring the Power of Positive Thinking

In our fast-paced and often challenging world, it's easy to get overwhelmed by stress, negativity, and self-doubt. However, amidst the chaos, there exists a transformative force that has the potential to change our lives for the better: positive thinking. The power of positive thinking extends far beyond mere optimism or wishful thinking. It is a mindset that can reshape our perception of the world, influence our actions, and ultimately shape our reality.

Positive thinking is more than just putting on a smile or ignoring life's difficulties. It involves actively choosing to focus on the positive aspects of our lives, cultivating an optimistic outlook, and approaching challenges with a solution-oriented mindset. Research in the field of psychology has increasingly recognized the significant impact positive thinking can have on our overall well-being and success.

When we embrace positive thinking, we open ourselves up to a multitude of benefits. By shifting our mindset, we invite happiness, resilience, and fulfillment into our lives. Positive thinking empowers us to navigate through obstacles, overcome setbacks, and persevere in the face of adversity. It has the potential to enhance our mental and physical health, improve our relationships, and even boost our performance in various areas of life.

In this article, we will delve into the fascinating realm of positive thinking and explore how it can profoundly influence our everyday lives. We will uncover the science behind positive thinking, provide practical tips and techniques to cultivate a positive mindset, and examine the ways in which positive thinking can impact our relationships within the family, among friends, and in the workplace. By understanding the power of positive thinking and implementing it into our lives, we can unlock a world of possibilities and create a brighter, more fulfilling future.

Join us on this journey as we uncover the transformative potential of positive thinking and discover how it can shape our lives in remarkable ways.

Understanding Positive Thinking: Definition and Benefits

Positive thinking is a mental and emotional attitude that involves focusing on the brighter side of life, maintaining an optimistic outlook, and actively seeking solutions rather than dwelling on problems. It is a conscious choice to shift our mindset towards positivity, even in the face of challenges and adversity.

At its core, positive thinking is about adopting a constructive and empowering perspective. It doesn't deny the existence of difficulties or dismiss negative emotions; rather, it encourages us to reframe our thoughts and interpretations, finding opportunities for growth, learning, and gratitude. By nurturing positive thinking, we develop a resilient mindset that helps us navigate life's ups and downs with greater ease.

The benefits of positive thinking are far-reaching and extend to various aspects of our lives. Here are some key advantages:

- ➤ Improved Mental and Emotional Well-being: Positive thinking has been linked to reduced levels of stress, anxiety, and depression. By focusing on positive aspects and cultivating an optimistic mindset, we enhance our overall mental and emotional well-being. Positive thinking promotes self-confidence, self-esteem, and a sense of empowerment.

- ➤ Enhanced Physical Health: Research suggests that positive thinking can have a positive impact on physical health. Optimistic individuals tend to engage in healthier behaviors, such as regular exercise, balanced nutrition, and adequate sleep. They also exhibit stronger immune system responses, lower blood pressure, and a reduced risk of cardiovascular problems.

- ➤ Increased Resilience: Positive thinking fosters resilience, allowing us to bounce back from setbacks and overcome challenges more effectively. It equips us with the mental strength and flexibility needed to adapt to difficult circumstances, learn from failures, and persevere in the pursuit of our goals.

> Improved Relationships: Positive thinking has a profound influence on our interactions with others. When we approach relationships with an optimistic outlook, we tend to radiate warmth, kindness, and empathy. This helps in building and maintaining stronger connections with family, friends, and colleagues. Positive thinking also promotes effective communication, conflict resolution, and teamwork.

> Heightened Creativity and Problem-Solving Abilities: Positive thinking stimulates creativity and enhances our problem-solving skills. When we maintain an optimistic mindset, we are more likely to approach challenges with a solution-oriented perspective, leading to innovative ideas and effective problem-solving strategies.

> Increased Success and Achievement: Positive thinking is closely tied to success and achievement in various areas of life. By focusing on positive outcomes and maintaining a belief in our abilities, we are more likely to set and pursue ambitious goals. Positive thinking fuels motivation, determination, and perseverance, which are key ingredients for accomplishing our aspirations.

In summary, positive thinking is a powerful mindset that holds the potential to transform our lives. By embracing positivity, we can experience improved mental and physical well-being, enhanced relationships, increased resilience, heightened creativity, and greater success. The journey towards positive thinking begins with a conscious choice and a commitment to nurturing a mindset that sees the best in ourselves, others, and the world around us.

The Science Behind Positive Thinking: How It Affects Your Brain

Positive thinking isn't just a feel-good concept; it has a scientific basis that can be understood through the study of neuroplasticity and the brain's response to different thought patterns. Emerging research in neuroscience has shed light on how positive thinking can profoundly impact the structure and functioning of our brains, ultimately shaping our thoughts, emotions, and behaviors.

Neuroplasticity, the brain's ability to reorganize and form new neural connections throughout life, plays a crucial role in understanding the science behind positive thinking. When we consistently engage in positive thinking, it triggers a cascade of neurochemical reactions and rewires the neural pathways in our brains.

One key area of the brain that is closely associated with positive thinking is the prefrontal cortex. This region is responsible for executive functions such as decision-making, problem-solving, and emotional regulation. Studies have shown that individuals who engage in positive thinking activities, such as gratitude exercises or positive affirmations, exhibit greater activation in the prefrontal cortex. This heightened activity is linked to improved cognitive flexibility, emotional resilience, and overall well-being.

Positive thinking also influences the release of neurotransmitters in the brain. When we maintain a positive mindset, our brains release chemicals such as dopamine, serotonin, and endorphins, which are associated with feelings of happiness, pleasure, and overall well-being. These neurochemicals not only improve our mood but also contribute to reduced stress levels and enhanced cognitive function.

Furthermore, positive thinking can dampen the activity in the amygdala, the brain's center for processing fear and negative emotions. By consciously focusing on positive thoughts, we can reduce the activation of the amygdala, leading to a decrease in anxiety and stress responses. This rewiring of the brain can have long-lasting effects on our emotional regulation and resilience in the face of adversity.

Research has also shown that positive thinking can enhance the connectivity between different regions of the brain, particularly those involved in emotional processing, memory, and social cognition. This improved connectivity allows for more effective communication between these regions, leading to better emotional regulation, stronger memory formation, and improved social interactions.

The effects of positive thinking are not limited to the brain alone; they extend to the body as well. Studies have demonstrated that positive thinking can have a positive impact on the immune system, leading to improved immune function and a reduced risk of certain illnesses. Additionally, the release of neurochemicals associated with positive thinking can contribute to lower blood pressure, improved cardiovascular health, and better overall physical well-being.

Understanding the science behind positive thinking reinforces its transformative potential. By consciously engaging in positive thinking activities, we can reshape our brains, strengthen positive neural pathways, and foster a more optimistic outlook on life. The brain's ability to adapt and change throughout life means that we have the power to rewire our thought patterns and cultivate a positive mindset, leading to a cascade of positive effects in our thoughts, emotions, and actions.

In the next sections of this article, we will explore practical tips and techniques for cultivating positive thinking and harnessing its benefits in our everyday lives.

Cultivating a Positive Mindset: Tips and Techniques

Developing a positive mindset is a transformative journey that requires conscious effort and practice. It involves training our minds to focus on the positive aspects of life, reframe challenges as opportunities, and nurture a resilient and optimistic outlook. Here are some practical tips and techniques to help you cultivate a positive mindset in your everyday life:

> Practice Gratitude: Regularly take time to reflect on and appreciate the things you are grateful for. This can be done through journaling, creating gratitude lists, or simply expressing gratitude verbally. Focusing on the positives in your life can shift your perspective and foster a sense of abundance and contentment.

> Positive Affirmations: Use positive affirmations to reinforce optimistic beliefs about yourself and your abilities. Repeat empowering statements that reflect your desired mindset, such as "I am capable," "I embrace challenges as opportunities for growth," or "I deserve happiness and success." Incorporate these affirmations into your daily routine, such as during morning rituals or before important tasks.

> Surround Yourself with Positivity: Surround yourself with positive influences, including uplifting books, podcasts, music, and supportive individuals. Engage in activities that bring you joy and inspiration. The environment we expose ourselves to greatly influences our mindset and outlook.

> Practice Mindfulness and Self-Awareness: Cultivate mindfulness by being present in the moment and non-judgmentally observing your thoughts and emotions. This self-awareness allows you to identify negative patterns or self-limiting beliefs and consciously choose to shift them

towards positivity. Meditation, deep breathing exercises, or mindfulness practices can aid in developing this awareness.

➢ Reframe Challenges: Instead of seeing obstacles as roadblocks, reframe them as opportunities for growth and learning. Embrace a "can-do" attitude and focus on finding solutions rather than dwelling on problems. By shifting your perspective, you can turn challenges into stepping stones toward personal development.

➢ Practice Self-Compassion: Treat yourself with kindness, compassion, and understanding. Avoid harsh self-criticism and negative self-talk. Celebrate your achievements, no matter how small, and acknowledge your efforts and progress along the way. Remember that self-compassion is essential in maintaining a positive mindset.

➢ Limit Exposure to Negativity: Minimize exposure to negative influences such as excessive news consumption, toxic relationships, or self-comparison on social media. Set boundaries and consciously choose to engage with content that uplifts and inspires you.

➢ Visualize Success and Positive Outcomes: Use visualization techniques to imagine yourself achieving your goals and experiencing positive outcomes. Visualize the steps you need to take and the joy and fulfillment that comes with success. This practice can boost motivation and reinforce a positive mindset.

➢ Practice Random Acts of Kindness: Engage in acts of kindness towards others, whether it's a small gesture or a significant contribution. Acts of kindness not only bring positivity into the lives of others but also foster a sense of fulfillment and gratitude within yourself.

➢ Practice Self-Care: Prioritize self-care activities that promote your physical, emotional, and mental well-being. Engage in activities that rejuvenate and recharge you, whether it's exercising, spending time in nature, pursuing hobbies, or connecting with loved ones.

Remember that cultivating a positive mindset is an ongoing practice that requires consistency and patience. Embrace the journey and be gentle with yourself as you navigate through challenges and setbacks. With time and dedication, you can develop a positive mindset that will transform your life and empower you to thrive in any situation.

Transforming Your Lifestyle Through Positive Thinking

Positive thinking has the power to transform your lifestyle and create a more fulfilling and joyful existence. By shifting your mindset and adopting a positive outlook, you can make significant changes in various aspects of your life. Here are ways in which positive thinking can help you transform your lifestyle:

- Improved Mental and Emotional Well-being: Positive thinking promotes mental and emotional well-being by reducing stress, anxiety, and negative thought patterns. It allows you to approach life's challenges with resilience and optimism, leading to greater inner peace and happiness.

- Enhanced Self-Confidence and Self-Esteem: Positive thinking nurtures a sense of self-belief and self-worth. By focusing on your strengths, achievements, and positive qualities, you can boost your self-confidence and improve your self-esteem. This newfound self-assurance enables you to pursue your goals and dreams with conviction.

- Healthier Relationships: Positive thinking positively influences your relationships with others. It enhances your ability to communicate effectively, express empathy, and cultivate harmonious connections. By radiating positivity, you attract positive people into your life and create a supportive social network.

- Increased Resilience and Adaptability: Positive thinking equips you with the tools to bounce back from setbacks and adapt to changing circumstances. It helps you view failures as opportunities for growth and learning, allowing you to persevere and thrive in the face of adversity.

- Enhanced Productivity and Motivation: A positive mindset fuels your motivation and productivity. By focusing on solutions rather than problems, you become more resourceful and goal-oriented. Positive thinking enhances your ability to concentrate, make effective decisions, and take proactive action towards your desired outcomes.

➢ Improved Physical Health: Positive thinking has a direct impact on your physical health. It reduces stress, which can contribute to better immune function, lower blood pressure, and improved cardiovascular health. Additionally, positive thinking promotes healthier habits such as regular exercise, balanced nutrition, and adequate sleep, all of which contribute to overall well-being.

➢ Increased Success and Achievement: Positive thinking opens doors to greater success and achievement. When you maintain an optimistic outlook, you develop a belief in your abilities and attract opportunities that align with your positive mindset. By embracing positivity, you unlock your potential and create a path to success.

➢ Greater Life Satisfaction: Positive thinking helps you appreciate the present moment and find joy in everyday experiences. It allows you to savor the beauty of life, cultivate gratitude, and find fulfillment in even the simplest of things. With a positive mindset, you can experience a deeper sense of satisfaction and contentment.

To transform your lifestyle through positive thinking, it is essential to practice and integrate it into your daily life. Embrace positive affirmations, gratitude exercises, and mindfulness techniques to reinforce positive thinking patterns. Surround yourself with supportive and positive influences, and consciously choose to focus on the good in yourself, others, and the world around you.

Remember, transforming your lifestyle takes time and effort. Embrace the journey, be patient with yourself, and celebrate your progress along the way. By incorporating positive thinking into your lifestyle, you can create a life filled with happiness, purpose, and endless possibilities.

Harnessing the Power of Positive Affirmations

Positive affirmations are powerful tools that can help reprogram your subconscious mind and shape your thoughts, beliefs, and actions. By consciously repeating positive statements, you can harness the power of affirmations to create positive changes in your life. Here's how you can effectively use positive affirmations:

> ➢ Identify Areas for Improvement: Start by identifying areas of your life where you want to create positive changes or develop a more positive mindset. It could be areas such as self-confidence, relationships, health, or success. Be specific about the qualities or outcomes you want to affirm.

> ➢ Formulate Positive Statements: Create positive affirmations that reflect your desired mindset or outcomes. Write them in the present tense, using "I am" or "I have" statements. For example, if you want to improve your self-confidence, affirmations like "I am confident and capable," "I believe in myself," or "I embrace challenges with confidence" can be effective.

> ➢ Make Them Personal and Meaningful: Tailor affirmations to resonate with your beliefs and values. Use words and phrases that have personal significance to you. This will strengthen the emotional connection to the affirmation and increase its effectiveness.

> ➢ Repeat Them Consistently: Consistency is key when using positive affirmations. Repeat them regularly, ideally multiple times a day. You can say them aloud, write them down, or even create visual reminders, such as sticky notes or digital affirmations on your phone or computer. Repetition helps reinforce the affirmation and embed it into your subconscious mind.

➢ Engage Your Senses: As you repeat your affirmations, engage your senses to enhance their impact. Visualize yourself embodying the qualities or experiencing the outcomes you are affirming. Feel the emotions associated with those affirmations and imagine how they positively impact your life. This multisensory approach strengthens the neural connections in your brain and reinforces the desired beliefs.

➢ Believe and Embrace the Affirmations: It's important to genuinely believe in the affirmations you are repeating. Cultivate a sense of faith and trust in their potential to manifest positive changes in your life. Embrace the affirmations as truths and align your thoughts, emotions, and actions with them.

➢ Combine Affirmations with Action: Affirmations work best when they are accompanied by action. Take inspired action that aligns with your affirmations and moves you closer to your desired outcomes. Use the affirmations as a catalyst for positive change and make choices that support them.

➢ Stay Patient and Persistent: Results may not be immediate, so be patient and persistent in your practice of positive affirmations. It takes time for your subconscious mind to absorb and integrate new beliefs. Trust in the process and continue affirming positive statements consistently.

Remember, positive affirmations are most effective when they are part of a holistic approach to personal growth. Combine them with other positive practices such as gratitude, visualization, self-care, and personal development to create a powerful foundation for transformation.

Harnessing the power of positive affirmations can empower you to reprogram your mind, overcome self-limiting beliefs, and create a positive mindset that aligns with your desired outcomes. Embrace the practice with dedication, consistency, and belief in the transformative power of your words.

The Role of Gratitude in Positive Thinking

Gratitude is a fundamental aspect of positive thinking that has the power to transform your mindset and enhance your overall well-being. It involves acknowledging and appreciating the positive aspects of your life, cultivating a sense of abundance, and focusing on the blessings and opportunities that surround you. Here's how gratitude plays a vital role in positive thinking:

> ➤ Shifts Focus to the Positive: Gratitude redirects your attention from what is lacking or negative in your life to what is present and positive. It helps you see the good in even the smallest things, fostering a mindset of abundance and appreciation. By consciously focusing on what you are grateful for, you train your mind to seek and recognize positivity in every aspect of your life.

> ➤ Enhances Positive Emotions: When you express gratitude, it generates positive emotions within you. Gratitude activates neural pathways related to happiness and well-being, releasing feel-good neurotransmitters such as dopamine and serotonin. By regularly practicing gratitude, you can experience increased feelings of joy, contentment, and optimism.

> ➤ Cultivates Resilience and Emotional Well-being: Gratitude strengthens your emotional resilience, helping you navigate challenges with a positive outlook. It allows you to reframe setbacks as opportunities for growth and learning, reducing stress and anxiety. By acknowledging the positives even in difficult situations, gratitude helps you maintain emotional well-being and cope with adversity more effectively.

> ➤ Improves Relationships and Connection: Gratitude has a profound impact on your relationships. When you express gratitude towards others, it strengthens the bond and

deepens your connection with them. Showing appreciation and gratitude for the people in your life fosters positive interactions, trust, and a sense of belonging. Additionally, practicing gratitude can help you cultivate empathy and compassion, leading to healthier and more fulfilling relationships.

➢ Promotes Mindfulness and Present Moment Awareness: Gratitude encourages you to be present and mindful. When you focus on what you are grateful for in the present moment, it anchors your awareness in the here and now. This mindfulness allows you to savor the beauty of life's simple pleasures and find joy in everyday experiences.

➢ Boosts Overall Well-being: Gratitude has numerous benefits for your overall well-being. Research has shown that practicing gratitude is associated with improved sleep, reduced stress levels, increased self-esteem, and a greater sense of life satisfaction. By incorporating gratitude into your daily life, you can experience a holistic improvement in your well-being.

➢ Strengthens Positive Thinking Patterns: Gratitude nurtures positive thinking by rewiring your brain to focus on the positives. As you consistently practice gratitude, you train your mind to automatically seek out and appreciate the good in your life. This positive thinking pattern becomes ingrained, making it easier to maintain an optimistic outlook even in challenging times.

➢ Enhances Personal Growth and Self-Reflection: Gratitude facilitates personal growth and self-reflection. By recognizing and acknowledging what you are grateful for, you gain insights into your values, priorities, and aspirations. It prompts self-reflection and helps you align your actions and choices with what truly matters to you.

Incorporating gratitude into your daily life can be done through simple practices such as keeping a gratitude journal, expressing gratitude to others, or reflecting on what you are thankful for. By consciously cultivating an attitude of gratitude, you can amplify the positive effects of positive thinking, foster a sense of fulfillment, and create a more joyful and meaningful life.

Overcoming Challenges with a Positive Mindset

Challenges are an inevitable part of life, but with a positive mindset, you can navigate through them with resilience, strength, and growth. Adopting a positive mindset allows you to reframe challenges as opportunities, overcome obstacles, and find valuable lessons in difficult situations. Here are strategies to help you overcome challenges with a positive mindset:

> Embrace a Growth Mindset: Adopt a belief that challenges are opportunities for personal growth and learning. Embrace the idea that you have the ability to develop new skills, overcome obstacles, and become stronger through facing challenges. View setbacks as stepping stones on the path to success rather than as roadblocks.

> Reframe Challenges as Opportunities: Shift your perspective by reframing challenges as opportunities for growth, self-discovery, and improvement. Instead of dwelling on the negative aspects, focus on the potential positive outcomes that can arise from overcoming the challenge. Look for silver linings and consider how the experience can contribute to your personal development.

> Cultivate Resilience: Cultivate resilience by developing the ability to bounce back from setbacks and persevere in the face of adversity. Build your resilience by practicing self-care, seeking support from loved ones, and maintaining a positive and determined mindset. Remind yourself of past challenges you have overcome and the strength you possess.

> Practice Positive Self-Talk: Monitor your internal dialogue and replace negative self-talk with positive affirmations and supportive messages. Remind yourself of your strengths, abilities, and past successes. Use empowering statements

such as "I can overcome this," "I am resilient," and "I have the skills to navigate this challenge."

➢ Seek Solutions: Approach challenges with a problem-solving mindset. Instead of dwelling on the problem, focus your energy on finding solutions and taking actionable steps. Break down the challenge into smaller, manageable tasks, and tackle them one by one. Celebrate each small victory along the way, as it will fuel your motivation and confidence.

➢ Practice Mindfulness and Self-Care: Engage in mindfulness practices to stay present and manage stress during challenging times. Take care of your physical, mental, and emotional well-being by prioritizing self-care activities that recharge and rejuvenate you. This includes getting enough rest, engaging in regular exercise, practicing relaxation techniques, and maintaining healthy habits.

➢ Draw on Past Experiences: Recall previous challenges you have successfully overcome and draw inspiration from those experiences. Remind yourself of the strategies and strengths you utilized in the past and apply them to the current challenge. Reflecting on past triumphs can instill a sense of confidence and remind you of your resilience.

➢ Surround Yourself with Supportive People: Seek support from family, friends, or mentors who can provide encouragement, guidance, and perspective during challenging times. Surrounding yourself with positive and supportive individuals can inspire you, offer fresh insights, and remind you that you are not alone in your journey.

➢ Focus on Solutions, Not Problems: Instead of fixating on the problems at hand, shift your focus to the solutions. Approach challenges with a proactive mindset and seek out opportunities for growth and improvement. Break down the challenge into manageable steps and take action towards finding solutions.

➤ Practice Gratitude: Maintain a grateful mindset even in the midst of challenges. Focus on what you are grateful for in your life, no matter how small. Practicing gratitude can shift your perspective, cultivate a positive mindset, and help you find hope and positivity in difficult times.

Remember, overcoming challenges with a positive mindset is a journey that requires patience, self-compassion, and perseverance. By embracing challenges as opportunities for growth and maintaining a positive outlook, you can develop the resilience and strength needed to overcome any obstacle that comes your way.

Building Resilience and Emotional Well-being

Resilience and emotional well-being are essential for navigating life's challenges, adapting to change, and maintaining a positive outlook. Building resilience allows you to bounce back from setbacks, cope with stress, and thrive in the face of adversity. Here are strategies to help you build resilience and enhance your emotional well-being:

- ➢ Cultivate Self-Awareness: Developing self-awareness is the foundation of building resilience and emotional well-being. Take time to understand your thoughts, emotions, and reactions to different situations. Recognize your strengths, limitations, and triggers. This self-awareness enables you to respond more effectively to challenges and make conscious choices that promote well-being.

- ➢ Develop a Supportive Network: Surround yourself with a supportive network of family, friends, and mentors. Seek connections with people who uplift and encourage you. These relationships provide emotional support, perspective, and a sense of belonging. Engage in open and honest communication with your support network, and don't hesitate to ask for help when needed.

- ➢ Practice Mindfulness and Stress Management: Incorporate mindfulness practices into your daily routine to reduce stress and enhance emotional well-being. Engage in activities such as meditation, deep breathing exercises, or journaling to cultivate present-moment awareness and promote a sense of calm. Prioritize stress management techniques that work best for you, such as engaging in hobbies, spending time in nature, or practicing relaxation techniques.

- ➢ Cultivate Optimism and Positive Thinking: Foster an optimistic mindset by focusing on positive aspects of your life, practicing gratitude, and reframing negative thoughts.

Challenge negative self-talk and replace it with positive affirmations and realistic optimism. Cultivating positive thinking patterns empowers you to approach challenges with resilience and maintain a positive outlook.

> Build Adaptive Coping Strategies: Develop adaptive coping strategies that help you navigate stress and challenges effectively. This includes problem-solving skills, effective communication, and seeking support when needed. Embrace healthy coping mechanisms such as exercise, hobbies, and self-care practices that nourish your emotional well-being.

> Embrace Change and Flexibility: Life is full of unexpected changes, and building resilience involves embracing them and adapting to new circumstances. Cultivate a mindset of flexibility and openness to change. See change as an opportunity for growth, learning, and new possibilities. Embracing change reduces resistance and enhances your ability to bounce back from challenging situations.

> Prioritize Self-Care: Make self-care a priority in your daily life. Take care of your physical, mental, and emotional well-being by engaging in activities that rejuvenate and recharge you. This may include getting enough sleep, eating a balanced diet, engaging in regular exercise, practicing relaxation techniques, and setting boundaries to protect your energy.

> Practice Acceptance and Letting Go: Foster acceptance of things beyond your control. Recognize that not everything can be changed or controlled, and focus your energy on what you can influence. Practice letting go of attachments to outcomes and surrender to the present moment. Acceptance frees you from unnecessary stress and allows you to channel your energy into productive actions.

> Learn from Setbacks and Failures: View setbacks and failures as opportunities for growth and learning. Reflect on the lessons you can extract from challenging experiences and use them to improve yourself. Embrace a growth mindset

that welcomes feedback, embraces mistakes as part of the learning process, and sees failures as stepping stones to success.

> Seek Professional Support if Needed: If you find it challenging to build resilience or manage your emotional well-being on your own, don't hesitate to seek professional support. Therapists, counselors, or coaches can provide guidance, tools, and resources to help you navigate challenges, process emotions, and build resilience effectively.

Building resilience and enhancing emotional well-being is an ongoing process that requires practice, self-compassion, and patience. By implementing these strategies into your life, you can develop the resilience and emotional strength to thrive in the face of adversity and lead a more fulfilling and balanced life.

Enhancing Relationships through Positive Thinking

Positive thinking not only has an impact on your personal well-being but also plays a significant role in fostering healthy and fulfilling relationships with others. By adopting a positive mindset and cultivating positive thinking patterns, you can strengthen your relationships and create a harmonious and supportive social network. Here's how positive thinking can enhance your relationships:

> Foster Optimism and Positivity: Positive thinking allows you to approach relationships with optimism and a positive outlook. It helps you focus on the strengths and positive qualities of others, fostering a sense of appreciation and gratitude. By maintaining a positive mindset, you create an environment that is conducive to open communication, empathy, and understanding.

> Practice Empathy and Compassion: Positive thinking encourages empathy and compassion towards others. It helps you see situations from different perspectives and understand the emotions and needs of those around you. By cultivating empathy, you can build deeper connections, offer support, and strengthen your relationships.

> Communicate Effectively: Positive thinking enhances your communication skills, enabling you to express yourself with kindness, respect, and clarity. It promotes active listening and encourages constructive dialogue. By adopting a positive mindset in your communication, you can minimize misunderstandings, resolve conflicts more effectively, and build trust with others.

> Encourage and Support Others: Positive thinking empowers you to be a source of encouragement and support for others. By recognizing and acknowledging the strengths and achievements of your loved ones, friends, and colleagues,

you foster a positive and uplifting environment. Your positive attitude can inspire and motivate others to reach their full potential.

➤ Build Trust and Resilience: Positive thinking helps build trust within relationships. When you approach interactions with optimism and assume positive intentions, it creates an atmosphere of trust and mutual respect. Additionally, positive thinking strengthens resilience in relationships, enabling you to overcome challenges together and bounce back from conflicts or setbacks.

➤ Cultivate Gratitude: Practicing gratitude within your relationships nurtures a positive and appreciative mindset. Expressing gratitude for the presence and contributions of others strengthens your bonds and creates a sense of warmth and connection. Regularly expressing gratitude can also help you navigate through difficult times, as it reminds you of the positive aspects within your relationships.

➤ Celebrate Successes and Milestones: Positive thinking encourages you to celebrate the successes and milestones of those around you. By rejoicing in their achievements, you create a supportive and uplifting environment. Celebrating together strengthens the bonds of your relationships and fosters a sense of joy and camaraderie.

➤ Resolve Conflicts Constructively: Positive thinking can help you approach conflicts in relationships with a constructive and solution-oriented mindset. It encourages you to focus on finding mutually beneficial resolutions rather than dwelling on negativity. By maintaining a positive attitude during conflicts, you can navigate them more effectively and preserve the harmony and well-being of your relationships.

➤ Practice Forgiveness and Letting Go: Positive thinking enables you to practice forgiveness and let go of past resentments or grudges. By embracing forgiveness, you create space for healing and growth within your relationships.

Letting go of negative emotions allows you to move forward with a positive and open heart.

➤ Be a Source of Positivity: Finally, positive thinking allows you to be a source of positivity in the lives of others. Your positive mindset and attitude can inspire, uplift, and influence those around you. By radiating positivity, you contribute to creating a supportive and nurturing social environment.

Remember that enhancing relationships through positive thinking is an ongoing process that requires conscious effort and practice. By adopting a positive mindset and incorporating these strategies into your interactions, you can cultivate fulfilling, supportive, and harmonious relationships with your loved ones, friends, and colleagues.

Strengthening Family Bonds with Positive Communication

Positive communication is the foundation for building strong and healthy family bonds. When family members communicate with positivity, empathy, and respect, it fosters a loving and supportive environment where everyone feels valued and understood. Here are some strategies to strengthen family bonds through positive communication:

➢ Active Listening: Practice active listening when engaging in conversations with your family members. Give them your full attention, maintain eye contact, and show genuine interest in what they have to say. Avoid interrupting and make an effort to understand their perspective before responding. Active listening demonstrates respect and fosters effective communication.

➢ Express Appreciation and Affection: Make it a habit to express appreciation and affection to your family members regularly. Acknowledge their efforts, accomplishments, and qualities that you admire. A simple "thank you" or a heartfelt compliment can go a long way in nurturing positive connections and strengthening family bonds.

➢ Use Positive Language: Be mindful of the language you use when communicating with your family. Choose words that are uplifting, encouraging, and respectful. Avoid negative or hurtful language that can create tension or strain in relationships. Positive language promotes understanding, openness, and a sense of safety within the family.

➢ Practice Empathy: Empathy is crucial in family communication. Put yourself in the shoes of your family members and try to understand their feelings and perspectives. Validate their emotions and let them know that you are there to support them. By showing empathy, you create an environment where everyone feels heard, understood, and accepted.

➢ Resolve Conflict Peacefully: Conflict is a natural part of family dynamics. When conflicts arise, approach them with a mindset of finding resolutions rather than assigning blame. Practice active problem-solving, focusing on the issue at hand rather than attacking each other personally. Encourage open and honest communication, and be willing to compromise and find common ground.

➢ Create Rituals of Connection: Establish regular family rituals that encourage positive communication and bonding. This could be a weekly family meal, game night, or designated time for sharing experiences and feelings. These rituals provide opportunities for family members to connect, strengthen relationships, and build trust.

➢ Practice Patience and Understanding: Family relationships can be complex, and it's important to practice patience and understanding. Be patient with each other's differences, quirks, and imperfections. Avoid making snap judgments or jumping to conclusions. Instead, seek to understand each other's perspectives and be willing to find common ground.

➢ Keep an Open Line of Communication: Maintain an open line of communication within your family. Encourage family members to express their thoughts, concerns, and needs openly. Create an atmosphere where everyone feels safe to share their feelings without fear of judgment or criticism. Regularly check in with each other and foster a culture of open and honest communication.

➢ Resolve Past Issues: Address unresolved issues from the past that may be affecting family dynamics. Engage in heartfelt conversations, practice forgiveness, and work towards healing and reconciliation. By addressing and resolving past issues, you create space for stronger and healthier family bonds to flourish.

> ➢ Spend Quality Time Together: Make a conscious effort to spend quality time with your family. Engage in activities that promote bonding, such as outings, shared hobbies, or family vacations. These experiences create lasting memories and deepen the emotional connection among family members.

Remember, building strong family bonds through positive communication is an ongoing process that requires effort and commitment from everyone involved. By incorporating these strategies into your family interactions, you can create a loving, supportive, and harmonious family environment where everyone feels valued and cherished.

Nurturing Positive Friendships: Support and Encouragement

Positive friendships play a vital role in our lives, providing support, companionship, and a sense of belonging. When we actively nurture and cultivate positive friendships, we create lasting connections that uplift and enrich our lives. Here are some ways to nurture positive friendships through support and encouragement:

- ➢ Be a Good Listener: One of the foundations of positive friendships is being a good listener. Show genuine interest in your friends' thoughts, feelings, and experiences. Give them your undivided attention and refrain from interrupting or judgment. By actively listening, you create a safe space for your friends to share and feel understood.

- ➢ Offer Support: Be there for your friends during both good times and challenging moments. Offer a lending ear, a shoulder to lean on, and practical assistance when needed. Show empathy, validate their feelings, and offer guidance or advice if appropriate. Knowing that they have your support can strengthen your friendship and foster a deeper sense of trust.

- ➢ Celebrate Achievements: Celebrate your friends' achievements, big or small. Whether it's a personal milestone, a professional success, or a personal growth moment, acknowledge and congratulate them. Celebrating their accomplishments demonstrates your genuine happiness for their achievements and reinforces the positive bond between you.

- ➢ Provide Encouragement: Offer words of encouragement and motivation to uplift your friends. Be their cheerleader in pursuing their dreams, overcoming challenges, or taking on new ventures. Your encouragement can boost their confidence, inspire them to reach their goals, and deepen your friendship.

➢ Practice Acceptance and Non-Judgment: Cultivate an atmosphere of acceptance and non-judgment in your friendship. Allow your friends to be their authentic selves without fear of criticism or judgment. Embrace their uniqueness, differences, and individuality. When your friends feel accepted, they are more likely to open up and be vulnerable with you.

➢ Show Appreciation: Express gratitude for your friends and the role they play in your life. Let them know how much you value their presence, their qualities, and the positive impact they have on you. Regularly express your appreciation through kind words, gestures, or small acts of kindness.

➢ Be Reliable and Trustworthy: Build trust in your friendships by being reliable and trustworthy. Keep your commitments, maintain confidentiality, and respect boundaries. Your friends should feel that they can rely on you in times of need, and that their confidences are safe with you.

➢ Offer Constructive Feedback: When your friends seek your advice or input, provide constructive feedback in a supportive manner. Be honest yet tactful, focusing on their growth and improvement. Help them see different perspectives and consider alternative approaches. Constructive feedback can deepen trust and contribute to personal and interpersonal development.

➢ Share Positive Experiences: Create opportunities to share positive experiences and create lasting memories together. Engage in activities that bring joy, laughter, and fun into your friendship. Whether it's trying new adventures, exploring shared interests, or simply spending quality time together, positive experiences create a strong foundation for your friendship.

➢ Be a Source of Positivity: Infuse positivity into your friendship through your attitude and actions. Be an uplifting and positive presence, offering words of encouragement, support, and optimism. Your positive energy will radiate and inspire your friends, creating a dynamic of mutual positivity.

Remember, nurturing positive friendships requires mutual effort and commitment. By incorporating these practices into your friendships, you can create a supportive and encouraging network that brings joy, growth, and fulfillment into your lives.

Positive Thinking in the Workplace: Boosting Productivity and Collaboration

Positive thinking has a profound impact on the work environment, influencing productivity, teamwork, and overall job satisfaction. When individuals maintain a positive mindset, it fosters a culture of optimism, resilience, and collaboration. Here are ways in which positive thinking can boost productivity and collaboration in the workplace:

➤ Increased Motivation: Positive thinking promotes a sense of motivation and enthusiasm among employees. When individuals approach their work with a positive mindset, they are more likely to be engaged, proactive, and committed to achieving their goals. This increased motivation drives productivity and encourages employees to go the extra mile.

➤ Enhanced Problem-Solving Abilities: Positive thinking enables individuals to approach challenges and obstacles with a solution-oriented mindset. It encourages them to focus on finding creative and effective solutions rather than getting stuck in negative thinking patterns. This optimistic approach enhances problem-solving abilities and fosters a culture of innovation in the workplace.

➤ Improved Communication: Positive thinking facilitates open and constructive communication among team members. When individuals maintain a positive attitude, they are more likely to listen actively, express themselves clearly, and provide feedback in a respectful and supportive manner. This positive communication enhances collaboration, strengthens relationships, and promotes a harmonious work environment.

➤ Increased Resilience: The ability to bounce back from setbacks and adapt to change is essential in the workplace.

Positive thinking cultivates resilience by helping individuals view challenges as opportunities for growth and learning. This resilience enables employees to navigate through setbacks, overcome obstacles, and maintain productivity in the face of adversity.

➢ Enhanced Teamwork and Collaboration: Positive thinking fosters a sense of unity and collaboration among team members. When employees maintain a positive mindset, they are more inclined to support and uplift each other, share ideas, and work together towards shared goals. This collaborative environment promotes synergy, creativity, and overall team effectiveness.

➢ Reduced Stress and Burnout: Positive thinking helps mitigate stress and prevent burnout in the workplace. When individuals adopt a positive mindset, they are better equipped to manage stress, maintain a healthy work-life balance, and prevent negativity from overwhelming them. This reduced stress levels and increased well-being contribute to higher productivity and job satisfaction.

➢ Boosted Employee Morale: Positive thinking contributes to a positive work culture and boosts employee morale. When individuals feel supported, appreciated, and valued in the workplace, they are more likely to be motivated, engaged, and satisfied with their work. This positive work culture fosters a sense of belonging and encourages employees to perform at their best.

➢ Increased Creativity and Innovation: Positive thinking stimulates creativity and innovation in the workplace. When employees approach their work with a positive mindset, they are more open to exploring new ideas, taking risks, and thinking outside the box. This mindset encourages the generation of innovative solutions, leading to continuous improvement and growth within the organization.

➢ Improved Customer Relationships: Positive thinking not only impacts internal dynamics but also has a positive influence on external relationships, particularly with customers. When employees maintain a positive attitude, it translates into positive interactions with customers, enhancing their experience and satisfaction. Positive customer relationships contribute to customer loyalty, repeat business, and overall organizational success.

> Enhanced Leadership: Positive thinking is instrumental in effective leadership. When leaders maintain a positive mindset, they inspire and motivate their team members, create a supportive work environment, and lead by example. Positive leaders foster a culture of trust, empowerment, and growth, which contributes to the overall productivity and collaboration within the organization.

In conclusion, positive thinking in the workplace has numerous benefits, ranging from increased productivity and collaboration to improved employee morale and customer relationships. By promoting a positive work culture and encouraging individuals to adopt a positive mindset, organizations can create an environment that nurtures productivity, innovation, and overall success.

Cultivating a Positive Work Environment

A positive work environment is essential for employee well-being, engagement, and overall organizational success. When employees feel valued, supported, and motivated, they are more likely to perform at their best and contribute positively to the workplace. Here are some strategies for cultivating a positive work environment:

- ➢ Foster Open and Transparent Communication: Encourage open and transparent communication throughout the organization. Create channels for employees to share their ideas, concerns, and feedback without fear of judgment or reprisal. Regularly communicate company goals, updates, and achievements to keep everyone informed and aligned.

- ➢ Lead by Example: Leaders play a crucial role in setting the tone for a positive work environment. Lead by example by demonstrating positive behaviors, such as respect, empathy, and gratitude. Show appreciation for employees' efforts, celebrate successes, and provide constructive feedback when necessary. Your positive actions will inspire and motivate others to follow suit.

- ➢ Encourage Collaboration and Teamwork: Foster a collaborative work environment where employees are encouraged to work together, share knowledge, and support one another. Encourage cross-functional collaboration and create opportunities for team-building activities. Recognize and reward collaborative efforts to reinforce the value of teamwork.

- ➢ Provide Growth and Development Opportunities: Support employee growth and development by providing opportunities for learning, training, and career advancement. Encourage employees to set goals and provide the necessary resources and support to help them achieve those goals.

When employees see a clear path for growth, they are more likely to feel motivated and engaged.

➤ Promote Work-Life Balance: Recognize the importance of work-life balance and encourage employees to maintain a healthy equilibrium between work and personal life. Offer flexible work arrangements when feasible, promote breaks and vacations, and discourage a culture of overworking. Supporting work-life balance contributes to employee well-being and reduces burnout.

➤ Celebrate Achievements and Milestones: Recognize and celebrate individual and team achievements, milestones, and successes. Acknowledge employees' contributions and publicly appreciate their efforts. Celebrating achievements fosters a positive and inclusive work culture, boosts employee morale, and reinforces the value of hard work.

➤ Create a Safe and Inclusive Environment: Ensure that the workplace is safe, inclusive, and free from discrimination or harassment. Promote diversity and inclusion by embracing different perspectives, backgrounds, and ideas. Encourage respect, empathy, and understanding among employees. Provide training and resources to create awareness and prevent biases or discriminatory behaviors.

➤ Encourage Wellness Initiatives: Support employee well-being by implementing wellness initiatives. Offer wellness programs, such as fitness challenges, mental health resources, and stress management workshops. Create a supportive environment that prioritizes employee well-being and encourages self-care.

➤ Emphasize the Importance of Feedback: Foster a feedback culture where constructive feedback is encouraged and appreciated. Provide regular feedback to employees to help them improve and grow professionally. Encourage employees to share their feedback, ideas, and suggestions for process improvement. Open and constructive feedback promotes continuous learning and improvement.

> ➢ Promote a Positive Work-Life Atmosphere: Infuse positivity into the work atmosphere by promoting a positive work-life atmosphere. Encourage humor, laughter, and camaraderie among employees. Organize social events, team-building activities, or recognition programs to foster a sense of belonging and positive relationships among coworkers.

Remember, creating a positive work environment is an ongoing effort that requires commitment from leaders and active participation from employees. By implementing these strategies, organizations can foster a culture of positivity, collaboration, and well-being, leading to increased employee satisfaction, productivity, and overall success.

Overcoming Negativity and Conflict at Work

Negativity and conflict in the workplace can have a detrimental effect on employee morale, productivity, and overall work environment. However, by taking proactive steps to address and overcome negativity and conflict, organizations can foster a more positive and harmonious workplace. Here are strategies for overcoming negativity and conflict at work:

> Foster Open Communication: Encourage open and honest communication among employees. Create a safe space where individuals feel comfortable expressing their concerns, frustrations, or conflicts. Encourage active listening and respectful dialogue to promote understanding and find constructive solutions.

> Address Issues Early: It's crucial to address issues of negativity or conflict as soon as they arise. Ignoring or allowing them to escalate can have a toxic impact on the work environment. Encourage employees to voice their concerns and ensure that appropriate measures are taken promptly to resolve the issues.

> Promote Empathy and Understanding: Foster a culture of empathy and understanding by encouraging employees to see things from different perspectives. Encourage individuals to put themselves in others' shoes and consider the impact of their words or actions. This empathy can help defuse conflicts and build stronger relationships.

> Provide Conflict Resolution Training: Offer conflict resolution training to employees at all levels. Equip them with the necessary skills to navigate and resolve conflicts effectively. Training should focus on active listening, assertive communication, negotiation, and finding win-win solutions.

➤ Encourage Collaboration: Encourage collaboration and teamwork to reduce negative competition and foster a cooperative work environment. Create opportunities for employees to work together on projects or cross-functional teams. Collaboration promotes shared goals, mutual respect, and can help alleviate conflicts that arise from individual differences.

➤ Establish Clear Expectations: Clearly communicate organizational values, behavioral expectations, and performance standards to all employees. When expectations are well-defined, employees are more likely to work together in a positive and productive manner. Regularly reinforce these expectations through feedback and recognition.

➤ Implement a Mediation Process: Establish a mediation process or designate a neutral third party who can help resolve conflicts. Mediation provides a structured and unbiased approach to conflict resolution. It allows employees to express their concerns and work towards mutually agreeable solutions with the assistance of a mediator.

➤ Encourage Positive Relationships: Foster positive relationships among employees by promoting team-building activities, social events, and opportunities for informal interaction. Encourage employees to build connections and get to know one another on a personal level. Positive relationships create a supportive and collaborative work environment.

➤ Lead by Example: Leaders play a crucial role in shaping the work environment. Lead by example by demonstrating positive behaviors, effective communication, and conflict resolution skills. Model respectful and constructive interactions with employees, and address conflicts promptly and fairly. Your actions set the tone for how others handle conflicts.

➤ Provide Resources for Stress Management: High levels of stress can contribute to negativity and conflict. Offer resources and support for stress management, such as employee assistance programs, wellness initiatives, or workshops on stress reduction techniques. Helping employees manage stress can mitigate potential conflicts.

➢ Celebrate Positive Interactions and Achievements: Recognize and celebrate positive interactions, collaboration, and achievements in the workplace. Highlight examples of employees resolving conflicts amicably or working together effectively. Celebrating positive moments reinforces a culture of positivity and encourages similar behaviors.

➢ Follow Up and Evaluate: Monitor the progress of conflict resolution efforts and assess the impact of implemented strategies. Conduct periodic evaluations to identify recurring issues and take proactive steps to address them. Regularly seek feedback from employees to gauge their perception of the work environment and identify areas for improvement.

By implementing these strategies, organizations can proactively address negativity and conflict, creating a more positive and productive work environment. Overcoming these challenges requires a collective effort from both employees and leadership, emphasizing respect, open communication, and a commitment to resolving conflicts in a constructive manner.

The Impact of Positive Thinking on Career Growth and Success

Positive thinking is a powerful tool that can significantly impact career growth and success. When individuals maintain a positive mindset, it not only enhances their overall well-being but also influences their professional journey in several ways. Here are some ways in which positive thinking can contribute to career growth and success:

> - Enhanced Confidence: Positive thinking boosts self-confidence and self-belief. When individuals have a positive outlook, they develop a stronger belief in their abilities and potential. This confidence enables them to take on new challenges, pursue ambitious goals, and seize opportunities for career advancement.

> - Increased Resilience: A positive mindset cultivates resilience, which is crucial for navigating obstacles and setbacks in the career journey. Instead of getting discouraged by failures, individuals with a positive outlook view them as learning experiences and opportunities for growth. This resilience allows them to bounce back quickly, adapt to change, and persevere in the face of challenges.

> - Improved Problem-Solving Skills: Positive thinking encourages a solution-oriented mindset. It enables individuals to approach problems and obstacles with a proactive and optimistic attitude. They are more inclined to seek creative solutions, think outside the box, and embrace challenges as opportunities for innovation and improvement. Effective problem-solving skills contribute to career success and open doors to new opportunities.

> - Stronger Networking and Relationship Building: Positive thinking enhances interpersonal skills and fosters positive

relationships in the workplace. When individuals maintain a positive attitude, they become more approachable, supportive, and collaborative. They build stronger networks, establish meaningful connections, and create a reputation as reliable and positive team players. These relationships can lead to mentorship, career guidance, and valuable professional connections.

➤ Increased Productivity and Motivation: Positive thinking promotes a sense of motivation and enthusiasm for work. Individuals with a positive mindset are more likely to be engaged, focused, and productive. They approach tasks with a can-do attitude, find joy in their work, and consistently strive for excellence. This heightened productivity and motivation contribute to career growth and advancement.

➤ Expanded Learning and Skill Development: Positive thinking encourages a growth mindset, fostering a thirst for knowledge and skill development. Individuals with a positive outlook actively seek opportunities to learn, grow, and acquire new skills. They embrace challenges, welcome feedback, and are open to continuous improvement. This commitment to personal and professional development positions them for career growth and advancement.

➤ Improved Leadership Abilities: Positive thinking is closely tied to effective leadership. Individuals who maintain a positive mindset exhibit qualities such as optimism, empathy, and resilience that are highly valued in leaders. Positive leaders inspire and motivate their teams, foster a supportive work environment, and lead by example. This leadership prowess opens doors to leadership roles and paves the way for career progression.

➤ Enhanced Job Satisfaction: Positive thinking contributes to higher job satisfaction and overall happiness in the workplace. When individuals maintain a positive mindset, they are more likely to find fulfillment and joy in their work. This satisfaction enhances their commitment, loyalty, and longevity within organizations. Content employees often attract new opportunities and promotions, leading to career growth.

> Improved Professional Reputation: A positive mindset contributes to a positive professional reputation. Individuals with a positive outlook are seen as reliable, proactive, and capable. Their positive attitude and approach to work earn them the respect and admiration of colleagues, supervisors, and clients. A positive reputation can open doors to new opportunities, referrals, and career advancements.

In conclusion, positive thinking has a profound impact on career growth and success. By cultivating a positive mindset, individuals can enhance their confidence, resilience, problem-solving skills, networking abilities, productivity, and job satisfaction. This positive approach sets the stage for continuous learning, leadership development, and the expansion of professional opportunities. Embracing positive thinking as a way of life can truly transform one's career trajectory, leading to greater fulfillment and success in the professional realm.

Instilling a Positive Mindset from an Early Age in Children

Instilling a positive mindset in children from an early age is a gift that can shape their outlook on life, their interactions with others, and their overall well-being. By teaching children the power of positive thinking, we equip them with valuable tools for navigating challenges, building resilience, and fostering healthy relationships. Here are some strategies for instilling a positive mindset in children:

> Model Positive Thinking: Children learn by observing their parents, guardians, and other influential adults. Model positive thinking by maintaining an optimistic attitude, expressing gratitude, and reframing challenges as opportunities. Show children that setbacks can be overcome and that a positive perspective can lead to better outcomes.

> Encourage Positive Self-Talk: Teach children to recognize and challenge negative self-talk. Encourage them to replace self-limiting thoughts with positive affirmations and empowering statements. Help them develop a strong sense of self-worth and teach them to approach themselves with kindness, compassion, and positivity.

> Focus on Strengths and Successes: Help children identify their strengths and celebrate their successes, no matter how small. Encourage them to recognize and appreciate their abilities and unique qualities. By focusing on their strengths, children develop confidence and a positive self-image.

> Teach Resilience: Resilience is essential for navigating life's challenges. Teach children that setbacks and failures are part of the learning process. Help them understand that resilience involves bouncing back, learning from mistakes, and trying again. Encourage them to view failures as opportunities for growth and personal development.

> Promote Gratitude: Teach children the value of gratitude by encouraging them to express appreciation for the people, experiences, and things in their lives. Encourage them to keep a gratitude journal, where they can write down things they are grateful for each day. This practice cultivates a positive outlook and fosters contentment.

> Encourage Positive Problem-Solving: Teach children to approach problems with a positive mindset and a solution-oriented attitude. Help them brainstorm creative solutions, encourage them to think outside the box, and emphasize the importance of perseverance. By teaching them that there are multiple ways to tackle challenges, children become more confident problem solvers.

> Foster a Supportive Environment: Create an environment that promotes positivity, kindness, and empathy. Encourage children to support and uplift one another. Teach them to be empathetic and to show compassion towards others. By fostering a supportive environment, children learn the value of positive relationships and the joy of helping others.

> Teach Mindfulness and Mindful Breathing: Introduce children to mindfulness practices that help them cultivate awareness of their thoughts and emotions. Teach them simple mindful breathing exercises to help manage stress and promote calmness. Mindfulness helps children develop self-regulation skills and enhances their ability to respond positively to challenging situations.

> Encourage Positive Social Connections: Teach children the importance of positive social connections and the impact they have on their well-being. Help them develop healthy friendships, practice effective communication skills, and encourage cooperation and teamwork. Positive social connections contribute to a sense of belonging and overall positivity.

> Celebrate Effort and Progress: Celebrate children's efforts and progress rather than solely focusing on outcomes.

Acknowledge their hard work, perseverance, and dedication. By recognizing and celebrating their efforts, children learn to appreciate the process of learning and grow a positive attitude towards personal development.

> Encourage Optimistic Thinking: Help children develop an optimistic mindset by encouraging them to see the bright side of situations. Teach them to reframe negative thoughts into more positive and realistic perspectives. Encourage them to approach challenges with optimism and a belief in their ability to overcome them.

Remember, teaching positive thinking to children is an ongoing process. Be patient, provide consistent guidance, and reinforce positive thinking practices. By instilling a positive mindset from an early age, we empower children to navigate life's ups and downs with resilience, optimism, and a sense of possibility.

Overcoming Obstacles to Positive Thinking

While positive thinking can have a transformative impact on our lives, there are certain obstacles that can hinder our ability to maintain a positive mindset. Recognizing and overcoming these obstacles is essential for embracing positivity and reaping its benefits. Here are some common obstacles to positive thinking and strategies to overcome them:

> Negative Self-Talk: Negative self-talk is a major obstacle to positive thinking. It involves the constant stream of self-critical and self-limiting thoughts that undermine our confidence and optimism. To overcome negative self-talk, practice self-awareness and challenge negative thoughts by replacing them with positive affirmations. Surround yourself with positive influences, seek support from others, and focus on your strengths and achievements.

> Fear and Anxiety: Fear and anxiety can consume our thoughts and prevent us from adopting a positive mindset. To overcome these obstacles, practice stress management techniques such as deep breathing, meditation, and mindfulness. Challenge your fears by gradually exposing yourself to what you fear, setting realistic goals, and reminding yourself of past successes and resilience.

> Pessimistic Thinking Patterns: Pessimistic thinking patterns, such as always expecting the worst or catastrophizing situations, can hinder positive thinking. Challenge these patterns by actively seeking evidence to the contrary, reframing situations in a more positive light, and focusing on realistic and balanced perspectives. Practice gratitude to shift your focus towards the positive aspects of life.

> Comparison and Envy: Constantly comparing ourselves to others and feeling envious of their achievements or

possessions can dampen our positive thinking. Overcome this obstacle by cultivating a sense of self-acceptance and gratitude for your own journey. Focus on your unique strengths and accomplishments, set meaningful goals for yourself, and celebrate the successes of others without letting it diminish your self-worth.

➢ Past Failures and Regrets: Lingering on past failures and regrets can create a negative mindset and hinder positive thinking. To overcome this obstacle, practice self-forgiveness and let go of the past. Learn from past mistakes, but don't dwell on them. Focus on the present moment and the opportunities it holds for growth and success.

➢ External Negativity: Surrounding ourselves with negative people, news, or media can make it challenging to maintain a positive mindset. Evaluate the influences in your life and minimize exposure to negativity. Seek out positive and supportive relationships, engage in activities that bring you joy, and choose uplifting and inspiring content to consume.

➢ Lack of Self-Care: Neglecting self-care can deplete our energy and make it difficult to maintain positive thinking. Prioritize self-care activities that nourish your mind, body, and spirit. This may include getting enough rest, eating nutritious foods, engaging in physical activity, practicing hobbies you enjoy, and spending time in nature.

➢ Fixed Mindset: Having a fixed mindset, believing that our abilities and traits are set in stone, can limit our potential for positive thinking. Cultivate a growth mindset by embracing challenges, viewing failures as learning opportunities, and believing in your capacity for growth and improvement. Embrace a mindset that recognizes effort, perseverance, and resilience as keys to success.

➢ Lack of Goals and Purpose: Without clear goals and a sense of purpose, it can be challenging to maintain positive thinking. Set meaningful goals that align with your values and passions. Break them down into actionable steps and celebrate each milestone along the way. Connecting with your purpose and focusing on the bigger picture can fuel positive thinking and motivation.

> Unrealistic Expectations: Setting unrealistic expectations can lead to disappointment and hinder positive thinking. Set realistic and achievable goals, and be compassionate with yourself if you encounter setbacks. Celebrate progress, no matter how small, and recognize that personal growth is a journey.

Remember that overcoming obstacles to positive thinking is an ongoing process. Be patient with yourself and practice self-compassion. With persistence and the right strategies, you can overcome these obstacles and cultivate a positive mindset that supports your well-being and success.

Cultivating a Sustainable Positive Thinking Practice

While embracing positive thinking is beneficial, it's important to cultivate a sustainable practice that becomes a natural part of your daily life. Here are some strategies to help you cultivate a sustainable positive thinking practice:

- ➢ Self-Awareness: Start by developing self-awareness about your thoughts and mindset. Notice when negative or self-limiting thoughts arise and consciously choose to replace them with positive and empowering ones. Regularly check in with yourself to evaluate your mindset and make adjustments as needed.

- ➢ Gratitude Practice: Incorporate a gratitude practice into your daily routine. Take a few moments each day to reflect on and express gratitude for the positive aspects of your life. This practice helps shift your focus to the things you appreciate, fostering a positive mindset.

- ➢ Positive Affirmations: Use positive affirmations to reprogram your subconscious mind and reinforce positive thinking. Choose affirmations that resonate with you and align with the mindset you want to cultivate. Repeat them daily, preferably in front of a mirror, to reaffirm positive beliefs about yourself and your life.

- ➢ Surround Yourself with Positivity: Surround yourself with positive influences, whether it's uplifting books, inspiring podcasts, supportive friends, or motivational mentors. Seek out environments that promote positivity and avoid negative or toxic influences that can hinder your progress.

- ➢ Mindfulness and Meditation: Practice mindfulness and meditation to cultivate present-moment awareness and detach from negative thoughts. Regular meditation helps calm the mind, reduce stress, and create space for positive thinking. Incorporate mindful moments throughout the day to check in with your thoughts and consciously redirect them towards positivity.

➤ Celebrate Small Wins: Celebrate your achievements, no matter how small they may seem. Acknowledge your progress and give yourself credit for the positive changes you're making. Celebrating small wins reinforces a positive mindset and encourages further growth.

➤ Learn from Setbacks: View setbacks as learning opportunities rather than failures. Embrace a growth mindset that sees challenges as stepping stones to personal development. Extract lessons from setbacks, adjust your approach, and use them as motivation to keep moving forward.

➤ Practice Self-Care: Prioritize self-care to nurture your overall well-being. Engage in activities that bring you joy, promote relaxation, and recharge your energy. When you take care of yourself physically, emotionally, and mentally, it becomes easier to maintain a positive mindset.

➤ Foster Supportive Relationships: Surround yourself with supportive individuals who uplift and encourage you. Seek out like-minded people who share your positive outlook and inspire you to grow. Cultivate meaningful connections and engage in conversations that promote positivity and personal development.

➤ Consistency and Persistence: Cultivating a sustainable positive thinking practice requires consistency and persistence. Make it a priority to practice positivity every day, even if it's just for a few minutes. Over time, these small efforts compound and become ingrained in your mindset.

➤ Reflect and Adjust: Regularly reflect on your progress and make adjustments as needed. Notice what strategies are working well for you and what areas need improvement. Be flexible and open to trying new techniques or approaches to enhance your positive thinking practice.

Remember, cultivating a sustainable positive thinking practice is a journey, and it takes time and effort. Be patient with yourself, embrace the process, and celebrate your progress along the way. With dedication and consistency, you can transform positive thinking into a lifelong habit that positively impacts every aspect of your life.

Conclusion: Embracing the Power of Positive Thinking

In today's fast-paced and often challenging world, the power of positive thinking is more important than ever. By consciously adopting a positive mindset, we can transform our lives and the lives of those around us. Positive thinking has the potential to shape our daily experiences, improve our relationships, enhance our well-being, and unlock our true potential.

Throughout this article, we have explored the definition and benefits of positive thinking, delved into the science behind it, and discussed various strategies for cultivating a positive mindset. We have seen how positive thinking affects our brains, influences our emotions, and contributes to our overall mental and physical well-being.

We have discovered that positive thinking is not about denying or ignoring the challenges and difficulties we face. Rather, it is about approaching those challenges with optimism, resilience, and a belief in our ability to overcome them. Positive thinking empowers us to reframe setbacks as opportunities for growth, maintain a sense of gratitude and appreciation, and foster a supportive and uplifting environment.

We have explored the impact of positive thinking on our relationships, both with our families and friends, as well as in the workplace. Positive thinking promotes effective communication, strengthens bonds, and fosters collaboration and productivity. It enables us to navigate conflicts with empathy and understanding, creating harmonious and fulfilling connections.

Moreover, we have discussed how positive thinking influences our personal growth, career success, and even the upbringing of children. By instilling a positive mindset from an early age, we lay the foundation for a lifetime of optimism, resilience, and well-being.

In conclusion, embracing the power of positive thinking is a choice we can make each day. It is a mindset that allows us to approach life's ups and downs with grace and gratitude. By cultivating a sustainable positive thinking practice, we can transform our lifestyles, overcome obstacles, and create a ripple effect of positivity in the world.

So, let us embrace the power of positive thinking, knowing that our thoughts have the potential to shape our reality. Let us choose optimism, kindness, and resilience as we navigate the journey of life, and inspire others to do the same. Together, we can create a world where positivity thrives, relationships flourish, and each individual can reach their fullest potential.